MW00937392

The
PRAYERS BEHIND
The
PERSON

The PRAYERS BEHIND *The* PERSON

Signed No Longer Scarred

INDIA FAITH

XULON ELITE

Xulon Press
2301 Lucien Way #415
Maitland, FL 32751
407.339.4217
www.xulonpress.com

© 2021 by India Faith

All rights reserved solely by the author. The author guarantees all contents are original and do not infringe upon the legal rights of any other person or work. No part of this book may be reproduced in any form without the permission of the author. The views expressed in this book are not necessarily those of the publisher.

Unless otherwise indicated, Scripture quotations taken from the King James Version (KJV) – *public domain.*

Printed in the United States of America.

Paperback ISBN-13: 978-1-66281-295-8
Ebook ISBN-13: 978-1-66281-296-5

This book is dedicated to Holy Ghost. Thanking Holy Ghost for remaining with me and in me despite making His stay Uncomfortable.

This book is dedicated to Jesus my Lord and Savior, Word, Example, Brother, and Friend for His love for the Father, for salvation, for interceding for me prior to leaving this earth. (Read John 17:6-26 and may it speak to your heart to remind you that Jesus had you in mind and He not only secured you through salvation, but He also secured you through prayer, and sealed you with Holy Spirit)

This book is dedicated to Abba Father, Lord what can I say!?! Or better yet what can I not say. You Alone Father make the impossible possible. You made an impossible creation possible. You laid the foundation of it all and then placed us in it. You set us in a prepared place, not just anything. You give thought to all things. So, while things are working together for our good because we love you and are the called according to your purpose you are positioning us for your expected end.

Thank you, Father, for loving what you created so much, valuing yourself so much that you saved us. Lord you are the true example of self-love. I say that because you created us in your image and likeness and despite the disruption you did not hand us over to satan. You fight for us and I thank you in Jesus name amen!

Introduction

This is not your ordinary daily devotional. This is not one you will find all orderly. This is for those who are or have experienced the tough side of life: out of order, out of sequence. This is to address those areas to bring order.

May the spirit of the living God convict your heart unlocking the wells of repentance to receive; willingly receive His wholeness, healing, reconciliation, love, and direction. Beyond that an encounter with Him that will take you from the curse place (Deuteronomy 28:15- 68) to His blessed place (Deuteronomy 28:1-14) through real salvation through Christ Jesus whom I proudly say is my Savior, Brother, Friend, Intercessor, and Present Help.

Hebrews 4:12-13 Speaks – For the word of God is quick, and powerful, and sharper than any two-edged, piercing even to the dividing asunder of soul and spirit, and of the joints and marrow, and is a discerner of the thoughts and intents of the heart. Neither is there any creature that is manifest in His sight: but all things are naked and opened unto the eyes of him with whom we have to do.

May we Capitalize on this Realization

What is life without death

What is growth without pain

What is strength without weakness

What is the value of Joy without sorrow?

What is the need of Jesus without

acknowledging eternal life?

To God be the Glory Forever and ever

and ever in Jesus name Amen!

Day One's Encouragement

(slight disclosure I have had plenty of day ones, as I believe we all do)

The power of where I am going is in God's hands and in my faith in Him. My faith in His call, my faith in His Purpose for my life, My Faith in His Person, and my Faith in His Choice of choosing me.

For I am God's choice and not his option. So, if God chose me why would I become subject to being man's option.

Day One's Prayer:

Lord I release it to you. I give you my thoughts and my feelings in Jesus name amen

Day One Teaching – Aug 6ᵗʰ, 2017

Exodus 20:13

Thou Shall Not Kill...

What comes to mind when you hear or read this scripture? Does the immediate come to mind? Well for me it did. People, we are not to kill one another.

However, what I believe to be implied here is beyond the obvious (BIG NO DO NOT KILL OTHERS, YOU DO NOT HAVE THE LEGAL RIGHT SPIRITUALLY OR NATURALLY TO TAKE THE LIFE OF MAN)

What about killing them within? Did you not realize there is more than one way to kill a person? The worst death I do not believe is the physical, but rather the spiritual, the mental, the emotional, the confidence of a man (human) when it dies.

What about that because those are the key components to living. There is living then there is being alive, vibrant, creative, taking control of your thought life, allowing God to lead you, being able to find the hidden treasures within you and being able to produce them into something tangible, Thriving!

Killing starts with the words we speak, or the words spoken by others. What is being deposited in you by what you are speaking and or what others are speaking into you?

As the word has spoken the power of life and death are in the tongue. We often use our words to destroy the ones we say we love the most, not expounding on their greatness, but exalting their weaknesses, their struggles, or their sins, based upon one's own judgments and opinions. Not realizing the heart of man (humans) is sensitive, it is to be protected. Yet the words of another serves as a bullet straight to one's soul.

That is a form of killing, so again the word of God states We shall not kill. In Jesus name amen

Day Two Encouragement -Speaking Life Into Me

Wake Up Wake Up Wake Up

Aug 13, 2017

Good Morning WAKE UP WAKE UP WAKE UP! This I say literally in the spirit realm. We often walk sleep or even dead, Arise from the death of this world and live. Be alive in Christ Jesus.

See this I write is not to you alone, but it was first to me. For how can one pull the beam out of another without first identifying that which is in their own. There has been so many in mine. Lies, false sense of self pride, the beast (sexual), unnatural desires (Jude 1:7), poverty, jealousy, envy, doubt, fear, lack of trust, idolatry, adultery, fornication, pornography, prostitution (whoredom), bitterness, submitting to the power and plan of the devil, backbiting, and there are still things God is bringing to the forefront to bring deliverance and freedom through my acknowledgement of these wrongs and surrender to His truth (the truth of the word of God) in Jesus name amen

Day Two - Teaching

What does one do when the beast return? When the disguise is not there, but it is present and in your face. Now that you are spiritually awake you see her, her whorish ways ready to consume your body to give it freely to someone else through sex and the release of penetration. To take over to give all of you to the men/women of the world. She is there to dwindle down your acknowledgement of God, to separate you in a way that causes you to no longer receive satisfaction from the things of God. Watch for her, for she is ready for the opportunity. Secure yourself through the word of God for it is the only weapon (the demons and demonic influences we must cast out requires us to be filled with the word, living in the word, and deeply submitted to God. There are NO breaks in abiding in the Lord, so He will abide in us and we may bear the righteous fruit. We must conquer death through life in Christ. His light must be that which pushes out the darkness within us) ***Please be reminded*** *that your flesh is alive with desires, and it is weak. That is why it is imperative that we must consecrate ourselves. For it is only through consecrating, prayer, fasting, studying the word of God, and speaking the word of God that will stop the power of this demonic spirit that desires to enter in and take over.*

1 Corinthian 6:15 Reminds us of this "Know ye not that your bodies are members of Christ? Shall I then take the member of Christ, and make them the members of a harlot? God forbid. What? Know ye not that he which is joined to an harlot is one body? For two, saith he, shall be one flesh. But he that is joined unto the Lord is one spirit. Flee fornication. Every sin that a man doeth is without the body; but he that committed fornication sinneth against his own body. What? Know ye not that your body is the temple of the Holy Ghost, which is in you, which ye have of God, and ye are not your own? For ye are bought with a price: Therefore, glorify God in your body, and in your spirit, which are God's.

Day Three - Parenting... Questions I ask myself as I evaluate my parenting 08/13/2017

What are your thoughts about your own children? Are you disgusted with them? Can they feel your disappointment in them because they have not nailed every area of life? Are you comparing them to your idea child or are you loving them right where they are?

Day Three Prayer

Father when I become annoyed let me correct me, and not allow annoyance to take precedence in the correction. For, that has a way of ruining our relationship and breaking communication between my children and I.

Day Three – The Talk

Let us be honest, at times we have these feelings listed above, but those should be brief, identified quickly, and controlled by your Spirit-man.

With our children temperance, longsuffering, are the two fruits we ought to share with our children. These fruits must be watered through the word and practiced in other spaces as well to allow them to grow bigger and bigger, for it will help us with our children. Our fruit must be ripe when sharing them with our children.

Repentance

Lord, please forgive me in the name of Jesus for every time I have allowed disappointment, anger, disgust, my own idea of a perfect child, and conquered my parenting. I ask that you cultivate and prune my garden. Where I bare the fruit of your spirit so I may use them with my children. Father I am at a new stage of parenting and I need your help. Lead me and show me how to surrender in Jesus name amen.

Galatians 5:22

But the fruit of the spirit is love, joy, peace, longsuffering, gentleness, goodness, faith, meekness, temperance. Against such there is no law (we need to apply all the fruit to our parenting. We must know which fruit to operate in at the appointed time. During this time temperance and longsuffering where the fruits I need to be pruned and nurture so that I could extend and share these fruits through my actions, speech, and interactions with them)

Day Four Prayer 10/26/2017

Lord I finally went for something greater than where I am, and all though I was shaking in my boots I did it trusting you.

Just because I was nervous does not mean that I did not trust God. Father applying for the Supervisor position was ground-breaking to a stagnant place that I have been. It shows I believe you have greater for me and I know this is just the beginning. In Jesus name amen!

Day Four – Teaching

Anytime you are measuring yourself by what the world requires versus what God is telling you to produce you are measuring wrong. See; the world requires you to produce based on what you have been taught.

But what God requires you to produce is based on what He has already placed inside of you. How He Himself has already wired you.

The world's system wants us to be mirrors and mimics of one another, but God encourages us, inspires us, and reminds us to stand in our own uniqueness.

We are one of a kind on purpose and remember just because you do not meet the measurements of the world systems does not mean you have failed. It does not mean you are inadequate. Remember you are in this world but not of it in Jesus name amen!

What it means is that you are purposed, and you have been blocked to redirect you to pursue it and walk in it fully.

Day Four Prayer

Dear Heavenly Father,

May we pursue you and not people. May we pursue purpose and not the worlds normal. May our hearts be so bowed to you that we are willing to risk it all, to take you at your word and be made new. May our hearts and minds rededicate its focus to you on purpose to fulfill purpose, to unite with purpose, to live in purpose. May our hearts cry out to you when we began to look like anything other than what you created.

I repent to you Father for allowing the worlds system to cause me to measure myself in accurately. My worth is immeasurable and those that are yours will willingly receive the wealth poured out through me by you in Jesus name amen.

A Thought that exposed the tactic of the enemy - Condemnation:

It is crazy because condemnation can be so subtle within. A little voice here or there.

You begin to praise God for what He is doing then a small voice or feeling comes to try to make you believe your praise is not worth it, make you feel your praise is not shifting things, or your praise is not accepted by God, or it is just downright silly.

Can you believe our Abba Father for New? Can you believe Him in the present moment that He is for you and not against you? Can you believe Him for what He desires to bestow on you? It is about His grace, mercy, favor, and love.

But remember as He exalts you it is for His glory alone and not yours or mans. I thank God that I am a recipient of His glory. Hallelujah!!! Amen

My God has the final say and I believe it to be Yes and amen in the name of Jesus...

Be Intentional

Everyday live with children included in the name of Jesus

Read to them and with them

Play games/ puzzles with them

Give them spelling words

Be there, attentive to their needs, and provide them with my undivided attention

Prayer:

Lord I will be present with Deauj'Zhane, Roman, and Jamal not how I see fit, but how you require in Jesus name amen

Father in the name

Day Five Teaching

John 3:27

A man can receive nothing unless it is given Him by Heaven

John 3:30

He God must increase, and I must decrease

John 3:32, 33

I receive the testimony of Jesus Christ and set to my seal that God is true. In Jesus name amen

John 4:1-3

Shows us Jesus did not fight every battle nor address every issue man had with Him. Once He was aware of an issue He departed in some instances. Wisdom!!! He separated Himself to stay on course with the will of God. We must mimic the same. Every fight is not worth fighting. Every argument is not worth proving your point. In the name of Jesus.

John 4:24

God is spirit... And we that worship Him must worship Him in Spirit and Truth...

John 4:32

But He (Jesus) said to them I have meat ye know not of.

John 4:34

Jesus saith unto them "My meat is to do the will of Him (God) that sent me, and to finish His work"

This lets us know we are not to get caught up with the daily common things of this world. We must understand that we are sent as well. Our fuel, satisfaction, and nutrition should be the call and will of our Father in Heaven. This should be the satisfaction and fulfillment of our hunger.

As the word has spoken man shall not live by bread alone but by every word that proceeds out of the mouth of God in Jesus name amen.

Day Five Prayer

Dear Heavenly Father,

I thank you for this day, another opportunity to follow you. I woke up to grace and mercy and your love shining on me in the name of Jesus. Father, I ask that you will forgive me of my sins that which I have committed knowing and unknowing in the name of Jesus. This day I decrease that you may increase. I surrender my will to you for your perfect Will to be lived out in my life that you may be glorified in the name of Jesus. Father there is nothing that I can receive unless it is given to me from Heaven. Lord, I desire what Heaven has for me. All things are spirit first. May I pray according to the Will of you Father that I may receive what Heaven has for me here on earth, that man may see your hand and know that you are real in the name of Jesus. May I be led by your spirit at all times. I declare I am going forth with the full armor on for I wrestle not against flesh and blood. I ask for your wisdom that I may know when to remove myself and when to fight according to the truth of your word and the mantle upon my life. I, India Faith set to my seal that God is true and the testimony of Jesus the Christ. May I dine with you and eat of your meat Father as I sit at the table you prepared for me in the name of Jesus. I commit myself to worship you in spirit and truth. Teach me your truth in the name of Jesus, expose every lie that I have believed. I bind the spirit of ignorance. May I stay close to you and study to show myself approved by you in Jesus name amen

Day Six When the Word Speaks

When the word speaks to you; Life comes to you

Zechariah 2:10

Sing and rejoice, O daughter of Zion: for I come, and I will dwell in the midst of thee saith the Lord! Hallelujah

Isaiah 54:1

Sing, O barren, thou that didst not bear; break forth into singing, and cry aloud; thou that didst not travail with child: for more are the children of the desolate than the children of the married wife saith the Lord

Isaiah 54:4

Fear not for thou shalt not be ashamed neither be thou confounded: for thou shalt not be put to shame, for thy shalt forget the shame of thy youth, and shall not remember the reproach of the widowhood anymore.

Joshua 17:17

And Joshua spake unto the house of Joseph even to Ephraim and to Manasseh saying, "Thou art a great people, and has great power, thou shalt not only have one lot"

In the name of Jesus this word is for you. This word is for you India Faith Signed No Longer Scarred

Day Six Self-Encouragement/ Prayer

I can do it! I can do more than one thing. God you are and will always be first in my life in Jesus name amen. Lord If I began to shift please correct me, give me an unction Holy Spirit, so that I am never out of order with you in the name of Jesus amen

Day six – Reminder

Matthew 7:11

If ye then, being evil know how to give good gifts to your children, how much more shall your Father which is in Heaven give good things to them that ask?

Matthew 6:30

Wherefore if God so clothe the grass of the field, which today is and tomorrow is cast into the oven, shall He not much more clothe you, O ye of little Faith.

Dear Heavenly Father,

I repent for the lack of faith. My prayer is that my faith will grow and that I believe you for the miraculous and for the impossible for all things are possible in you in Jesus name amen.

Holy Spirit Reminded Me Nov 12, 2017 @ 12:07am

In the absence of man rescuing me God rescued me!!! It is so in Jesus name amen. And, I would have it no other way.

~ Signed No Longer Scarred ~

India Faith

Day Seven – How Do You Wait

How do you wait? Do you wait, discouraged or encouraged? I have had my moments of encouragement and discouragements while waiting. But we must hold the deposits God has placed on the inside of us. Trusting Him at all cost. Being assured that what God has spoken and ordained in our lives shall come to pass.

It is funny as one begins to grow and mature in God you really understand that there is nothing more important than Him, and what He has to say. You begin to be released from the pressures of all that you thought mattered. Show me oh God, mature me Oh God in the name of Jesus amen.

Day Seven

We spend so much time trying to feel our prayer when in fact we should spend our time believing. What is your posture in prayer? Even if you do not feel it, are you willing to believe it because God's word says it?

While you patiently wait on the Big request you are seeking the Lord for, do not forget to bless Him and be attentive and grateful for the in between. The other blessings and deposits God is adding to you for they are just as big as your special request, and worthy to give God praise in Jesus name amen

Lord I thank you for my gift card in the name of Jesus. It is such a blessing to have received it. It is a simple reminder that I am favored by you. Daily I will wait and live with my expectations in you in Jesus name amen

Day Eight Reminder 11/16/2017

Never give more of yourself to what you are paid to do than to what you are ordained to do.

You are ordained by God, so give excellence in everything. In Jesus name amen

Day Eight Prayer

I am praying to know and understand your love language towards me Father God in the name of Jesus amen.

Day Eight Declaration

I will no longer live a lazy life

I will stop being lazy with my life

I will enjoy my time on earth within the parameters God has made available

I will no longer extend myself, because of the need of money

What is in me that I am to offer to this world?

What are you saying to me today Lord, in this month, in this season? What are you saying to me right now Lord in the name of Jesus amen?

I choose to Trust You Abba in the name of Jesus Amen!

Day Nine 11/26/2017

My experience as a parent, be ready for the unexpected. Do not allow the unknown to torment you. Take it all to God.

We honestly do not know what each day will look like nor the next moment, but we do understand and know that all things will be good, because it works together for our good in Jesus name amen.

In His arms we can delight and take refuge in Jesus name amen.

Day Ten - Song 11/27/2017

Oh, how I love you, oh how I adore you, oh how I worship you, for alone you are my God. Hallelujah

Day Ten – 11/28/2017

Fights, Murmuring, Arguments come from within. We ought to pursue peace within which allows us to pursue peace with others despite our differences

Be aware of your emotions and do not allow them to rule, influence or dictate your actions and or interactions with others

Do not wage war on another based on how you are feeling. Never trust feelings when you are in a negative state. Pay attention to what is being spoken in your mind to create those feelings.

Learn to communicate and express yourself without hardness. Stern and yet with a tone one can accept. Communication is everything. How far are you able to go without respectful communication?

Let nothing steal your peace within. Learn not to become annoyed by other actions, or by the way they carry themselves, etc.

Learn to be genuine. Ask God for help in Jesus name amen.

Day Eleven – Prayer

Dear Lord,

Good Morning to you this day Father God, good morning Jesus, good morning Holy Ghost. The Son has risen on our behalf this day, and because you have risen my seeds and I have also risen. We are not bound to death. We have life and life abundant. Lord you are everything to me in the name of Jesus. Thank you for keeping us safe. Lead us and guide us this day. Please order our footsteps in Jesus name amen.

Let me open my eyes each day to give of myself and to receive my portion in Jesus name amen. Father I need a stripping of a lazy spirit. Wake Up I say to myself. Father God lead me in the name of Jesus. I bind poverty. When my eyes open Lord let me wake up. Allow my spirit man to wake up inside of me in Jesus name amen

Father, thank you for thinking of me this day! Thank you for pouring your word, assurance, encouragement, and love in me this day. I am anointed, and you are in control please order my footsteps in Jesus name amen.

Day Eleven – Teaching

John 8:12

Then Jesus spake again unto them saying "I AM THE LIGHT OF THE WORLD" Here Jesus tells us exactly who He is. This also implies in the world without Him we are consumed in darkness. Darkness in our hearts, our minds, our spirit, and our souls. Jesus exposes the darkness in our lives to give us the ability to exchange darkness for His light. That the brightness of His light as He shines through us will draw man to come. In the name of Jesus amen.

Instructions – follow me (Jesus) in Jesus name amen

Reward/Benefit – You shall have the light of life and shall not walk-in darkness in Jesus name amen

The In between – My talk with God

Over the past few months, extended weeks I have felt alone, uncertain, and shaking within my natural self. Fear had consumed! Father God if you alone did not lift me this day 12/17/2017 I do not know what would have taken place. You sent your word to me by a man of faith to encourage me to pursue you, to just keep my faith, and seek your will which is your Kingdom. He also explained (reminded me) to keep my eyes fixed on you and your Kingdom. This was so reassuring for me. Please continue to give me an ear to hear. Forgive me for my strong feelings against my child's father allow me not to get in the way of their relationship.

This day Father I ask for your wisdom and truth to speak to me through me and guide me in the name of Jesus. What is truth saying to me currently? Your truth Father please guide me. I lift the anxiety, worry, fear to you and I speak peace within my mind and unto my child as well in the name of Jesus.

I leave all my anger and frustration, concerns, and the disrespect I feel and or felt on this paper and I declare a release within. Father, I pray your spirit will abide with my child and let him have a great time. Let him feel comfortable, please protect him, and do not allow any bad seeds to be planted in the name of Jesus amen. I let go and I divorce his father's spirit, and anything attached that would cause me to care in a way that the behavior displayed would negatively impact my person. Please bless him and his family in Jesus name amen.

Lord the gentleman I met explained how your promises to me will come to pass. He shared his testimony about what the doctor said. It ignited my faith to declare that my Father shall live and Not die in the name of Jesus for you alone are in control of it all in Jesus name amen

Day Twelve – Thoughts and Reminders

I live my life unto God for self not for anyone else.

When I buy something, it is to bless my home not because someone else is watching. I am living my best life. My children are living their best lives in Jesus name amen.

Thank you for causing me to drop to my knees to pick up a pen in the name of Jesus amen

It will all work out: My new life, financial freedom. Yay!!! Thank you, Father God this bankruptcy option is an available option, in Jesus name amen.

I am not adopting anyone else's perspectives. I am learning God's perspective and it is His perspective that is changing my views, opinions, judgements, decisions, and thought process in Jesus name amen

Day Twelve Prayer

Dear Lord,

Please create in me a clean heart, so that I will worship you. Purify me for only the pure in heart shall see you Father God.

This day I turn from my wicked ways, but in my heart, I still know the lie of my pay day and rent is still there, and I know that I am going to move forward with the lie Lord please forgive me in the name of Jesus. Righteousness let it not be mere words that I speak let my actions, behavior, character follow Father here I am surrendered to you. Let me be a true example of an unconditional follower of Jesus Christ our Lord and savior. This year search my heart and deliver me from the ills of my soul. I honestly sense new. Not just Natural, but spiritual. New Kingdom Reality, New Perspective, New Hope, New Light, New Cry, New Song, New Worship, New Yes, New Obedience, Real Obedience Developed without Limitations. Please show me where my children and I belong in the house of God on earth and what house in the name of Jesus amen.

Day Thirteen – Written by No Longer Scarred

The Heart of me... The heart of me; Father I am broken, and I just cannot sleep. I cannot sleep because I need you to come and heal me. As I am believing you for the impossible, the limitation comes to combat my faith and trust in you, but I declare I cannot stop, I must press through. As I sit here to try and write this daily devotional of substance that I have prewritten simply trying to put it together I just cannot contain. Contain the fact that my writing to you is free flowing in the moment. In the times of my hearts cry. I cry out to you for I know that you will respond. I know that you answer, and I know that you care about every tear. Lord as I am stepping into this new territory to possess the land, to live out my latter end it has been mentally challenging. The pressure of uncertainty tries to consume me. Yet in all of this I know in my heart you are for me, so in that who and what can be against me. I say it but I still feel the pressure of the opposition. I choose not to let go of your truth. I choose to follow you where you led. My life is not my own and I am soooooooooo extremely tired of toggling between what was and what is to be. Fighting against the old me trying to allow the new me, the real me, the authentic me emerge. The me that is created in the image and likeness of God.

You see I have been touched from the beginning almost as if the plot to destroy was against me when I took my first breath. Satan had a plan, but God always had a new beginning. Touched but not burned, broken but reconstructed into a masterpiece by the master himself.

The Lord has gifted me to release my heart's cry to Him, to capture it on paper and for so many years I have held on to it. Held on to the gift and talent and I cannot even say I know or understand why. As I released my tears to Him tonight, I said I will not bury my talent. Lord show me how to be a great steward and multiply my talent, in addition Lord please help me discover the many more. What I am understanding is often we cannot access the more until we develop the one. This night I repent to you Father in the name of Jesus for being so selfish. For not being able to see past myself. The Lord is maturing me. I am not saying that to say I am childish in my character by any means when dealing with and interacting with man (humans). This morning 11/30th at 4:12am as I laid and processed all that was before me. I spoke with God. I was looking for a home, and I believe He has allowed me to locate it. Here is the problem and where I had to repent. When Holy Spirit exposed an area where I needed to grow, because I cannot allow the enemy to have any access to me. Once I felt the release and confirmation from Abba regarding our home immediately, I was lifted. It was like ok I am cool. It was an unlocking of something within that freed *me to pray, trust and the block was removed. I do not like it. It reminded me of one of my children being cool when they know you are going to give them what they want. I did not realize that behavior was in me. The Lord told me He was taking me by a way that I know not and let me tell you He is doing just that. He is exposing because I am growing. My heart says Lord grow me know matter what. Show me the ugliest parts of me. Let your light expose the darkness within me. You know the word is working in your life when it shows you, you! You know your heart desires more of Jesus and to be more like Jesus when you can accept what He shows you and it brings you to repentance. See this may seem small to some and we override it, but this is huge. We need the Lord to get down in the crevices of our character to deal with the hidden things.*

You know I Lord I hate satan. He frustrates me so much. I know He is not my problem God has taken care of Him. But I think about how he uses us as people, lie, manipulate, tempt, distract, abuse, and destroy so many. I pray Dear Heavenly Father please give us eyes to see, a heart that loves you with all our spirit, all our soul, and all our might. With every fiber of our being draw us to repentance daily. Make us all aware, self-aware.

I must admit I do not have it all together. I need the Lord every second of every minute. I literally cannot breathe without Him, I cannot think straight without Him, for I am nothing without Him.

I utterly understand why the Lord says to walk in the spirit. For when we walk in the spirit, we remain untouchable. Walking in the spirit and dwelling in the secret place of the Highest as we abide in the shadow of the Almighty then and only then when the weapons formed, they shall not prosper, because we are in our hiding place. I must ask myself this question... India Faith, who told you to come out of hiding? We must remember our lives are hidden in God with Christ. Our salvation holds weight. It gives us access to life. See when we do not have salvation and we do not feel as if anything in our lives is wrong, we will never understand how right life in Christ is. Nor understand the value of salvation. I pray for all who may not only read, but if you even have touched this book may you have an encounter with the savior.

When He knocks open

When He call answer

For the day you hear His voice harden not your heart. In Jesus name I pray amen

What I love about God He perfect us through our broken-ness. Through our willingness to admit to Him we have no idea of what we are doing and what life is all about. When we say Lord, I need you, Father I want you just as much as I know that I need you and where I lack a desire for you Dear Heavenly Father give me the desire. I desire to desire you Lord, to follow you, to read your word, to study and understand your word, so your word, life, and light may become alive in me. See we need the word of God to be alive in us for there are times in our walk, and relationship with the Father we are unable to speak the word, and we need the word to speak to us. We need the word to uplift us and encourage us for in our weakness His strength is made perfect. In order for the word to speak to us, and in order for the word to speak through us we must get it inside of us by reading, studying, and delighting ourselves in His word. For when we delight in His word, we delight in Him. God is beautiful! He gave us earth, He prepared the place prior to our arrival (all we had to do was maintain it, we are responsible for the upkeep) then he created the physical body of man to dwell here on earth, disruption came (major disruption so many times) the Lord said I am going to give them a Savior Jesus (God) for salvation (allow you to choose Him through your free will) secure and leave those that are mine with Holy Ghost (God), and on top of that I am going to leave you a bible which is a tool to live. I am going to show myself to you through this bible, I am going to give you instruction, and tell you the reward of your obedience. To be honest I find myself in the bible often. For it is definitely the breath of God. Not only that for me I know it is real and the word of God is life, because when I speak it back into my own life, I feel His spirit, His anointing, His light, and life through.

I stand on Hebrews 4:12-13 because it is real and true.

"We do not succeed until we realize how rich we really are. When we begin to understand the riches, we possess are eternal. They are everlasting and it is within us. 2 Corinthians 4:7 But we have this treasure in earthen vessels, that the excellency of the power may be of God, and not of us.

Day Fourteen

Even now I am on a journey, and I am on an assignment. My assignments are a part of the journey. It all will come to God's expected end for my life. For the thoughts God thinks of me are good and not evil.

Signed No Longer Scarred

India Faith

Day One (again)

Be careful what you speak into your life. As a little girl innocent, yet not innocent through exposure of pornography I spoke prostitution. I used to take my brother's tank tops and make them into a skirt. I clearly remember me saying I was going to be a prostitute. I did not realize the power that I possessed, but in this now moment of reflection I see it oh so well. I did not realize who I was in the eyes of God. I was ignorant to the fact that what I spoke was creating my soon to be reality I prophesied over my life. The problem was I prophesied the wrong thing out of my mouth. I now am prophesying life, the right things over myself. I declare and decree I am a minister on behalf of the Most High God. I was called into the Kingdom of God prior to birth, as we all are! I declare I am making money the right way. I am anointed. I am at peace. I love myself. God is happy with me. I am mature in the things of God. I am disciplined in all areas of life. I am an excellent mother. I am a profound book writer. I am a profound speaker. I am called to preach the gospel of Jesus Christ. I have the spirit of Living God in me who gives me power to tread upon serpents and scorpions, and over all the power of the enemy, and I can stand on it for nothing shall by any means hurt me in Jesus name amen (Luke 10:19) He has chosen me to heal the sick and raise the dead in the name of Jesus. I am healed mentally, physically, emotionally, and spiritually. I literally owe no man nothing, but love. God takes pleasure in me. I am a worshipper. The things of high importance in my life. God is first, and head of my life, my home, my children, my decisions. I believe the word of God. I live by the word of God, I have revelations from God, I share daily the word of God with my children. I am the head and not the tail. I am above only and not beneath. I am debt free. I am a lender and not a borrower In Jesus name amen (we speak those things that are not as though they were. We are created to speak what the word says. Not what circumstance speaks to us. We must drown out the noise of what we see and begin to speak God's reality in the name of Jesus amen) *I do not seek attention. I am satisfied with myself, and I am enough. I get to choose who I will say yes to according to the will of God. I am not chasing, people, status, things, nor position. For Father in*

Heaven the main source in my life, you are currently positioning me, and I will be in full throttle momentarily. It is my time in Jesus name amen for your glory to be revealed in me. My coming forth party my date has arisen. It is time to celebrate. Lord let me not attempt to force anything. Everything about me looks so different. Now is the time in Jesus name amen.

Day Fifteen – Declaration of the Word of God

Philippians 4:6-7

I, India Faith will be anxious for nothing, but in everything by prayer and supplication with thanksgiving I will make my request known unto God and the peace of God which passes all understanding shall keep your hearts and minds through Christ Jesus. In Jesus name amen!

Matthew 7:7-8

Ask and it shall be given you, seek and ye shall find, knock and it shall be opened unto you. For everyone that asketh receiveth, and he that seeketh findeth, and to him that knocketh it shall be opened in Jesus name amen!

John 14:13-14

And whatsoever ye shall ask in my name, that will I do, that the Father may be glorified in the son. If ye shall ask anything in my name I will do it says the Lord

Father in the name of Jesus I am asking to receive a yes for this current supervisor position that I have interviewed for. A yes from you and man. This day 10/29/2017 I am making my request known unto God that I not only want to be the answer to their problem, but I am asking for your grace and peace to fulfill the requirements of the role. I am making this request through prayer and supplication with thanksgiving unto you Father God. Your word decrees if I ask, I shall receive If I seek, I will find. I am seeking you Father God for this position and not self-seeking or seeking man, by faith I am knocking, and it is opened to me according to your word. Even with me asking, I also ask that you bless my mind with vision, clarity of thought, and the capacity to use the fullness of my brain Father God. Your word says whatsoever I ask in the name of Jesus he will do it for me so that He may be glorified our Father God. So, this prayer I submit to you in Jesus name amen

Sincerely,

Signed No Longer Scarred

India Faith

Now Faith is the substance of things hoped for and the evidence of things not seen. In Jesus name amen!

May I take a moment to explain no matter how hard I prayed, used scripture I did not get the position. One of the greatest lessons in this is that what we are asking for must be according to the will of God. I do not recall asking if this position was His will for my life. If fulfilling this role was written in my journey. Despite the company going with another candidate, I believe two or three different times. I did not curse God. I remained professional and moved forward. Even though we do not understand it the Lord never want us to get complacent. In retrospect I would have for sure. Thank you, Jesus for the No's, in my life for it pushes me forward in the things you have pre-destined for my life. I have no more time to waste time in Jesus name amen.

Day sixteen - Prayer

Today Lord I surrender people to you those that are in my life. I ask for wisdom Father God to place them in a level of priority no one ever ranking above you nor drawing me out of your presence. Positioning, I pray for wisdom in their positions in my life. In the manner they stand in regard to importance to my relationship ministry to you.

Father I pray for your wisdom in discerning the spirit, and the intentions of those who are in my life. No matter their face. Lord I pray for instructions on how to take inventory

Day Seventeen – Teaching/Prayer/Encourager (Seek Jesus) 12/02/2020

In order to live you must die! To live you must die. The word of God says in order to gain life you must be willing to lose your life. It says those who hold on to their lives will lose it, but those who are willing to lose their lives will gain life in Christ Jesus. Be encouraged this day! May you be the one that is willing to lose what you thought was life, to lose your own thought process, your own agenda, and how you see yourself. Begin to seek the Father for life in Christ Jesus to be about your father's business, to learn of his agenda for your life, to surrender it all to him, to give a pure yes from within. Do you want it? Yes, you want it! You hunger, you thirst for it. You know that there is an emptiness inside of you that you want to be filled, but you just cannot figure it out. What is it? This is because your soul longs for Jesus, your longs for Jesus. Your soul longs for the nurture and nourishment that he gives to you when you follow Him. May the eyes of our understanding be enlightened on this day! God is for you and because He is for you then who can be against you. Oftentimes: it is us, ourselves that are against our own selves, and that is causing so much damage within and it is a reflection in our lives. May we continuously see ourselves the same way

God sees us. The Lord is for us, He will help us, He will heal us. He will lead you to life more abundantly in the name of Jesus amen.

Day Seventeen – The Release I needed to Get it OUT (sometimes we must get it out, verbally to break the spiritual barricades that are formed against you. We war with our mouth by speaking the word of God)

You know the funny thing about moving forward is that oftentimes it feels as if you are moving backwards. God's way is beyond our ways. Our minds cannot even begin to comprehend or fathom the process of His thoughts. We must be so intentional and incline our ears unto him and as we incline our ears unto Him by listening intently and in a way, we are listening to receive we position ourselves to hear and the Lord said when we hear that is when our soul lives. My God My God My God I thank you in abundance for who you are. I thank you for your love for my life. I thank you that you have never let me go. I thank you that you constantly breathe into me, in me, and upon me. YHWH you are YHWH hallelujah I am so glad to be yours. My soul belongs to you, I am your territory in the name of Jesus, my children belong to you, they are your territory in the name of Jesus. I do not care what things look like. I do not care what things feel like. What I do know is I care about being in right standing with you Abba Father!

I care that my heart, my mind, my spirit, and my soul is always saying yes to you Hallelujah Jesus. I am redeemed and set free! I thank you Lord for being my refuge. I thank you Lord for being my fortress. I thank you Lord for being my strong tower. I thank you Father God for being my way maker. You are Jehovah Jireh. I always have more than enough in the name of Jesus amen Hallelujah. I give you all the glory, all the praise, and all the honor in Jesus name amen! Be encouraged, be lifted up, speak life into yourself, do not side with the way that you are feeling, do not side with your circumstances and how things look. Begin to fix your eyes on Jesus, begin to fix your eyes on Him alone in the name of Jesus amen.

Day Eighteen - Lord let's talk, how are you?

What is my reality? Please allow me to see through the eyes of you. I bind all that attempts to come against my mind. My choice today is to see and think clearly. Allowing myself the space to be, be all the me that I am. I choose you this day. I thank you Father because what I see is that my life, and my timing is on a different wave link than others. I appreciate the waves, they are peaceful and comforting. I am so grateful! I must admit although things can be daunting; during this time, I am truly ecstatic about where I am! Trade it absolutely not, not for nothing. I invite you to walk with me and guide me through each step of my life moving forward. I am happy about your choice in me and calling me forth at your appointed time. I have had some real moments recently facing me.

This weekend I have space, space just to be. I cannot wait to see their faces tomorrow Roman and Jamal. I love them and look forward to seeing DeaujZhane in December.

Day Nineteen: Prayer Scripture Reminder

Ok, let me tell you! I have been on this journey with God and He has called me to a place that I know not of. It is unfamiliar and if I may be so honest, I have been all over the place in my feelings, emotions, conversations within.

Who is this woman I see when I look at me! Beauty, Boldness, Confidence, Power, Authority, Gracefulness, Love, Faith, Wisdom, Strength. A Woman that cannot be stopped and will not be stopped. In the name of Jesus amen

Day Twenty

Let No one get in the way

May we run our race in confidence and assurance

Let us let go of everything that ties us to the old man

The old way and the old life

For in Christ old things ways mindset are gone and all things have become new

We are not bound to man let me say that again We are not bound to man

No longer can anyone speak to us in the manners in which they once did

Do not be so quick to accept things from people, discern their spirit. You do not want to taint God's blessing by receiving something from anyone God has not ordained.

To all be encouraged and remember the road is not easy but it is not tough for God has already gone before us in the name of Jesus amen.

Again, let us not be overly sensitive to others and disregard what the Lord has called us to say and do.

I declare and decree we are not afraid of men and their faces in the name of Jesus amen

I declare and decree that courage is rising up this day

I declare and decree that confidence is rising up this day

I declare and decree that every chain is broken this day

I decree and declare that Boldness have taken over this day

I decree and declare that the Lion of Judah is roaring inside of Us in the name of Jesus amen

Because Jesus who is the Lion of Judah lives in us

I decree and declare Genesis 49: 8-12

"Men and Women of God, your brothers will praise you; your hand will be on the neck of your enemies; your father's

sons will bow down to you. You are a lion's cub, Judah; you return from the prey, my son.

Like a lion he crouches and lies down, like a lioness— who dares to rouse him? The scepter will not depart from Judah, nor the ruler's staff from between his feet, until he to whom it belongs shall come and the obedience of the nations shall be his (Jesus). He will tether his donkey to a vine, his colt to the choicest branch; he will wash his garments in wine, his robes in the blood of grapes.

His eyes will be darker than wine, his teeth whiter than milk" (Genesis 49:8-12).

May I encourage you with the word of the Lord this day

Revelation 5:5

'Do not weep! See, the Lion of the tribe of Judah, the Root of David, has triumphed. Because He Triumphed, we Triumphed! We must know who is inside of us in the name of Jesus amen

He alone is able to open the scroll and its seven seals'" (Revelation 5:5).

Our confidence is not in ourselves; our confidence is not in man, but our confidence must be in the Lord in the name of Jesus amen

I pray this word is inscribed upon the tables of your hearts this day for in our God and in this truth is where our freedom lies so again

as Isaiah 2:22 has spoken Cease ye from man, whose breath is in his nostrils: for where is he to be accounted

In Jesus name amen!

Day Twenty One - Prayer

Dear Heavenly Father,

I am coming to you with the weight and burdens of my financial state. The lack of wisdom, stewardship, and discipline I have shown.

I ask for you to forgive me Lord for miss handling, miss using, and robbing you in tithes, offerings, and seed for my own gain despite the consistent results of it being to my own demise and lack.

Lord this day I come to you to repent of my known wrong and financial abuse and carelessness. I am coming to you Father to ask you to evaluate and search my heart for I know there are things still there that would trigger misuse. I ask for deliverance from the lack of wisdom, knowledge, discipline, and self-control. Please uproot what I have learned based on what I have seen and done in the past and allow Holy Spirit to teach me.

(Great Revenue) Be it unto me as Holy Spirit has spoken.

Although I am not emotional my carnal mind wants to say I do not believe what I am asking for. I REBUKE YOU SATAN, CARNALITY AND EVERY SELF SABOTAGING THOUGHT. I DECLARE THE TRUTH OF GOD'S PROMISE WHICH IS THE MIND OF CHRIST IN JESUS NAME AMEN

PHILIPPIANS 2:5 Let this mind be in me India Faith which was also in Christ Jesus

In Jesus name amen

I know Father that you are the one that gives me the power to get wealth. Deuteronomy 8:18

Based on your word you can do exceedingly abundantly above all that I can ask or think according to the power that worketh in me. Ephesians 3:20 (wisdom, knowledge, understanding, faith, belief)

Dear Heavenly Father, through the abode of the Holy Spirit please let me know how to access the power that worketh in me. Reveal to me what the power is in me and how to live in and work my power in the name of Jesus amen. For your glory and my freedom in Jesus name amen

The earth is yours and the fullness thereof. I know that we are to be your demonstration in the earth. You have not

called us/ me India Faith to poverty. Your word says your
hand is not shortened. Isaiah 59:1

YHWH, I do not fully understand, but I ask Holy Spirit
to teach me. I lay my burdens at your feet and ask that you
will pick them up and stop the plan of destruction I created through ignorance, disobedience, selfish desires, and
a lack of trust.

Ask of you Lord, I India Faith ask of you Lord to trans-
form me from these ailments and impoverished conditions
in the name of Jesus.

I thank you this day for allowing my heart, and mind to
be honest and open about this condition. I look to the hills
from which cometh my help. My help cometh from the You
Lord which made Heaven and earth in the name of Jesus
amen. Be it unto me as you have willed in my life Psalms
121:2 amen

Mark 11:23 Be thou cast into the sea, all forms of debt in
the name of Jesus amen

I decree and declare from this day forward I am a good
steward, from this day forward I will not owe another
person, another business another enemy, another nothing
in the name of Jesus amen.

For I am free indeed and Free indeed (William Murphy)
made this plain in my mind in my will, how I feel in
Jesus name amen

Day Twenty Two

Dear Lord,

I pray that I do not end bad. I pray that my children do not end bad. Lord, please allow me to dig deep and show my children how to dig deep, so we are self-aware. So, we can walk through the door You opened and be relentless.

Lord let me teach my children how to fight. So, we will reach our land. Our land flowing with milk and honey. We must fight the things within that block us from your best in the name of Jesus amen.

My children and I will place our feet on what you have preordained in the name of Jesus amen.

God, you have already worked out what I am worried about.

Day Twenty Three 07/23/2020

Subtle Distractions

Father at this moment I am struggling. One part of me is saying I do not know and another part of me is saying yes you do.

A double minded man is unstable in all their ways.

I declare and decree I am of one mind committed to proceed with purpose. I honestly believe I must be purged. I must literally separate myself from my phone for the next few days.

I find myself going on Facebook to see what has been posted. What has been said. Trying to see who texted me and none of that is important.

What is really important is that you are trying to speak to me. What is really important is that I position myself at your feet to hear.

You love me like in a way unheard of. When I am in this state it is crippling then I rethink the importance of swift execution. For a moment of being wanted by man above the desire of being wanted by You Father God. Man's desire for us is temporary God's desire for us is eternal and I want it. I repent for sacrificing your love and direction for something not real. In the name of Jesus amen

Why would I continue to hold on to a pond? It is time to let go and receive my King!

In my weakness maybe that is the best time to release what God has said. In those moments maybe that's when strength is re-established and regained in my life in Jesus name amen.

Dear Father,

I thank you for breath, life, correction, and your word speaking to me directly.

How do I live blameless?

Please condition my heart to be blameless in your sight in Jesus name amen.

Lord you appear unto us. Please appear unto me. I need daily encounters with you in the name of Jesus amen

Do not become a pillar of salt due to disobedience; because you must have one more look, one more taste, one more touch, one more smell. Because you must fornicate one more time, lust one more time, lie one more time, rebel one more time. It will cost and are you able to pay the cost?

There are consequences

Dear Heavenly Father I want to freely be submitted and used by You through yielding my free will to your perfect will on my way to Heaven.

I do not want to be used by You, speak of you on my way to hell. Take away the stony heart Lord and give me a heart of flesh in the name of Jesus. Put a new spirit inside of me in the name of Jesus amen

Day Twenty Four 12/28/20

Today is a little heavy but I am deciding to press. At moments we do not even know or understand where the weight is coming from. Today there is a little sadness and despite me going through a huge transition I feel the sadness and sorrows of other people. So, I lift my hands and my heart to the Lord this day and proclaim His name Emmanuel – The Lord is always with us. Lord let us feel your presence. Those who are of a heavy heart a sad countenance let lift up their eyes so they can look to the hills from which comes their help. Their help comes from you Lord even when they do not know it. Even when it is not realized. How can I love past fault to be there for someone else? Let us learn to not take an account for a suffered wrong. But be merciful, be kind, be tender, mourn with those that mourn, and have a heart for people. Lord those that are in need and hurting visit them today. Speak to them is such a way that they catch your voice through all the noise and the sound that plague their mind and bombard their thoughts. Jesus my heart cry out for your tender mercy for those in need. As a matter-of-fact Abba we are all in need, so I cry out for humanity we are hurting. We are plagued, we are suffering, confusion is at an all time high and we have disregarded your truth I repent for us as a nation. I repent for our very soul. Dear Heavenly Father please have mercy on us for we know not what we do. For those who are earnestly seeking you and may not know the way send someone please put a stop to satans hands and evil desire. How Lord, how can I help turn the nations heart back to you, what is my sphere of influence to bring thy Kingdom come thy will be done on earth as it is in Heaven. Life is failing in front of our eyes and we still walk blind despite the destruction we see that is dead smack in our face. Heavenly Father I stand corrected for you alone are life, so life itself is not failing but the lifeline of this world and its system is. You alone are the way the truth and the life. Me individually, I am a part of your remnant, I ask how do I stand up? How do I posture myself to bring glory to your Kingdom, to set the captive free, to release the broken hearted? Send me I will go! Do I know what going looks like? No. Do I know where going is? No. But send me I will go. I trust you in the name of Jesus

Those who are yours need you and I cry out to you this day. Everyone is not yours, but yours need you Heavenly Father. Angels of the living God I need you to come out, I need you to fight for us. I ask you of you Heavenly Father to send them to battle on our behalf that the souls of your people are free. May we your children rise up and see what we have never seen before. May our hope rise, and our spirit glisten for the Lord strong and mighty in battle has come

I speak life right now in the name of Jesus this day every plan the enemy has set to destroy a life prematurely turn it around Father. Those who ran out of your grace Lord please give them another chance Dear Lord we need your mercy. Please do not consume us in your fury but remember us again. In the name of Jesus amen

Day Twenty Five

Today I am showing up exactly where I am. I am embracing my emotions, I am embracing the subtleness of my very being, and allowing the departure to take place. I am ok, I am good, and I am on the right path to victory. In this moment I am relaxing my mind, refusing the chaos, and declining all thoughts that are not true, lovely, honest, pure, just, or of a good report. I embrace the peace of God, for Jesus said He leaves me his peace, not as the world giveth but He gives it unto me.

I was left instructions and so were you. I am instructed through the word of God if I keep my mind stayed on Him, I will remain in perfect peace.

Today I surrender. I surrender everything that I thought I was and everything I thought I was not. Today I exchange my life for the new life in Christ Jesus. Today I open my spiritual ears, and heart to the sound, the sound of Heaven speaking to me. The host of Heaven has invited me in, and I cannot be late. Here I am Father God here I am in the name of Jesus. I have my oil; my lamp has not gone dim. My heart cries out for you and my soul bow down to you as you receive me for your glory. Here I am Lord Here

I am Lord my very person is humbled and filled with so much honor to you for waiting on me until I could get it right within my soul. You have so much grace and mercy, and I have been a true recipient of it daily. You loved me through my wrong and held me through my hurt even when it was self-inflicted through disobedience. Who is like a God unto you no one? There is no one who can stand before you. There is no one who can set their eyes on you for you are way too glorious in the name of Jesus amen

Day Twenty Six

Life – You are way to glorious. We spend our time trying to figure you out vs trying to get to know You. Life you are way too complicated to consume in our thoughts, your being is too vast to jot it all down. It takes a lifetime just to get to know You – Life

Life- I thank you for extending yourself to me, simply being the air that I breathe and the thoughts that I think. I thank you life for showing up and extending my days even when death wanted to come and take me to my grave. Did I deserve life, did I take care of life, did I show life

that I appreciate even being a thought that came into existence to be on a planet called earth along with other vessels? Who in some cases truly do not know how to appreciate life or know exactly who life is.

Thank you for introducing yourself to me Life you are my newfound friend, you are the one who has been assigned to me to teach me to live (read Proverbs 8) There is so much beauty in you I look forward to discovering. Now that I am submitted to You under your blood I am covered. Life is wisdom, Life is God, Life is Jesus only through life can one stand tall.

Life I am glad to get know you and I will no longer spend the rest of my days trying to figure you out, but embrace every moment, going no moment without in Jesus name amen

Day Twenty Seven 04/13/2018

Father Good Morning, I thank you for the air that I breathe this day! My hope is in you Lord in Jesus name amen.

Show me your face I want to see you; I want to see your glory I want to live in your secret place show me your face (William McDowell) This is my hearts cry this day and William McDowell expressed it well in song in the name of Jesus amen

Father God I am excited about You. I am excited about us! You are continuously making my day in the name of Jesus amen.

I am excited to live in a place of truth, purity, and honesty continually. Lord fill us, please in the name of Jesus amen.

Draw your people forth and together to be of one mind, the mind of Christ in the name of Jesus amen.

Time to silence the house from television, devices to cleanse the atmosphere. Father I no longer want to wake up worn out by dreams, etc. I speak your peace over my mind through the night hours in the name of Jesus

Today Lord I surrender people to you. Those that are in my life, I ask for wisdom Father God, to place them in a level of priority. No one ever ranking above you or drawing me out of your presence in the name of Jesus amen

Positioning I pray for wisdom in positioning them in the manner they stand regarding importance to my relationship and ministry to you.

Father I pray for your wisdom in discerning the spirit, and intentions of those who are in my life. No matter their face. Lord I pray for instruction for instructions on how to take inventory of the people I am presently connected to. I pray I understand why and if the connection and or relationship does not serve a purpose for you. If it pulls from me vs adds to me, please show me how to cut it. Please remove it. No more self-inflicted hindrances in the name of Jesus amen.

(Grow me through my parenting in the name of Jesus amen I have the grace I do)

Day Twenty Eight

I repent for becoming desensitized to your spirit, desensitized to your presence, desensitized to your leading, and desensitized to your voice. I repent for not remaining in your way, for drifting off into an unknown way however a way that was never too far for you to find me.

Dear Heavenly Father I thank you for finding me. I thank you for what you are doing in my life at this moment. Restoring our relationship so that your oil, your anointing, your word will flow. I never want to be one that performs, and then be distant from you. Every time I get up to speak and come down from speaking may I remember why I do, and may it be because I absolutely love and adore you, because I absolutely appreciate you my Promiser more than the promises, because I absolutely honor He who is life more than the life I live. On this day may I bear my cross that you may be glorified in the name of Jesus amen. May you purify my love, respect, reverence, fear, and honor toward you. May my life be one that is based off of a listening ear, and an immediate response to obey.

I believe the God I serve, the God who loves me is walking me step by step day by day. I hear His voice for I am His sheep and I follow Him in the name of Jesus amen

I need the fullness of you Lord operating in my life, and the lives of my children. Correct, rebuke, love, relationship, use, mold, shape, and be glorified in our lives in Jesus name amen.

Always show me and my children where we are in you, and correct our course in Jesus name amen. I bow my life to You Abba (Father, Son, Holy Ghost) in a sweet surrender. Have your way in Jesus name amen

Day Twenty-Nine

Father, my Abba Father I need your help, wisdom, patience, love, compassion, as I raise Roman and Jamal. Your love to cover a multitude of sin, your compassion to love past behavior or what I feel may not be right behavior. I need your wisdom to correct them and teach them of you. Your patience to spend time, provide individual attention, and be present and interact with them. Father, I need your help to walk me through parenting two boys. Without self-getting in the way and negative emotions that attempt to consume us as parents when our children behave in a way that is not ideal. In the name of Jesus allow me to see the best and speak the best over their lives. May I correct them always out of love and please forgive me for correcting them out of frustration at times. May I correct them out of love alone in the name of Jesus amen.

Father both Roman and Jamal belong to you. Their heart and soul are yours. They are great, smart, wise, geniuses. I declare they are confident and whole. They can do all things through Christ who strengthens them. Please show them who they are and will be in Jesus name amen~

I see myself as an adult and not a kid. I am fearless and not fearful. I trust you Lord in Jesus name amen.

I thank you for calming my spirit.

Day Thirty

Please help me focus on what is going on with me. All the noise I hear around me please let me be so focused and in tune with our relationship that I am not easily distracted.

I bind the noise. I can only live my life. I am going after my life in the name of Jesus. The life given to me through Christ in Jesus name amen. I cannot live no one's life other than my own. Lord in the name of Jesus I desire to walk with you. Through my daily interactions I am doing necessary work yet still allowing myself to be lost in You in the name of Jesus amen. Committing my works unto You Lord so that my thoughts are established.

Day Thirty-One

04/16/2018

Dear Heavenly Father, My Abba Father, my real Father please teach me how to agree with you in all your ways and in all my ways. Because two can only walk together peacefully when they agree. I pray Lord that you agree with my character, conversations, actions, and what I believe. My prayer is that I am right in your site. May I always agree with your correction. With an open heart receive your corrections. For it is with gratitude understanding that you correct me because you love me in the name of Jesus amen.

Abba you are the owner of me, and I accept and own who I am in you without regret, and without hesitation in Jesus name amen.

Father it is you alone whose ways are not mine and your thoughts far excels mine. I know that there is a way that seems right to man but the end thereof leads to death. Lord let my motives become a mimic of yours according to the measure of life you have given. Purity should be the beat of my heart, for your word declares only the pure in heart shall see God (Matthew 5) I India Faith desire to see You! I desire to see you daily in my thoughts, my atti-tude, my actions, my words, the things I pursue and that which I shy/steer away from. I need to see you in it all in Jesus name amen.

This here, our relationship is real! I am a vessel unto honor. I choose life, I surrender to God in the name of Jesus amen.

Like, I am totally excited God; that I am a God carrier. You really live, reside, and rest in me. Wow I am completely honored and desire to only please you. Keeping my flesh clean for my body is your temple. Look at that, you created temples to reside in on earth that you can dwell in; live in which creates that one on one personal, intimate relation-ship. I am in awe of You God. We as humans we do things and know not, but you do things and know. I love you and my heartbeats, because of you and for you in the name of Jesus. I say yes Amen!

Psalms 40:8

I delight to do thy will, O my God. Yea thy law is written in my heart in Jesus name amen!

I Am

I am called by God

I am created for the Master's use

I am anointed by God himself

Through Christ Jesus I am saved

God has sanctified me

I have been endowed with the comforter Jesus left for me, so I would not be alone

The Holy Ghost of God lives in me, and intercede for me

He reveals to me the things of God

He unctions me, reveal, guide, and inspires me

I can do all things through Christ

My Abba has made His abode in me

I am kept

My children are kept (Deaujzhane, Roman, Jamal)

Dear Lord,

I thank you this day, I love you this day, and invite you to take full control. Wherever my soul, mind, spirit, flesh, would or will rebel I surrender my free will to you to take control. Do what you have to do Father in the name of Jesus amen.

Signed no longer Scarred

India Faith

CPSIA information can be obtained
at www.ICGtesting.com
Printed in the USA
BVHW080809270521
608292BV00004B/610